31 BEST PRACTICES

VOLUME II

EVERY TRAINER SHOULD KNOW

DAN'L ADAMS

authorHOUSE®

AuthorHouse™
1663 Liberty Drive
Bloomington, IN 47403
www.authorhouse.com
Phone: 1 (800) 839-8640

Published by AuthorHouse   11/17/2015

ISBN: 978-1-5049-6052-6 (sc)
ISBN: 978-1-5049-6051-9 (e)

Library of Congress Control Number: 2015918777

Print information available on the last page.

Any people depicted in stock imagery provided by Thinkstock are models, and such images are being used for illustrative purposes only. Certain stock imagery © Thinkstock.

This book is printed on acid-free paper.

31 BEST PRACTICES

VOLUME II

EVERY TRAINER SHOULD KNOW

DAN'L ADAMS

authorHOUSE®

AuthorHouse™
1663 Liberty Drive
Bloomington, IN 47403
www.authorhouse.com
Phone: 1 (800) 839-8640

Published by AuthorHouse   11/17/2015

ISBN: 978-1-5049-6052-6 (sc)
ISBN: 978-1-5049-6051-9 (e)

Library of Congress Control Number: 2015918777

Print information available on the last page.

31 Best Practices Every Trainer Should Know (Vol. II). Why Volume II? When I was a kid I thought if I ever became a rock star, my first album (big black vinyl circular thing with grooves played on a thing called a record player) would be Dan'l's Greatest Hits (I played trombone at the time), thinking that if I was successful, people would want to find my previous albums... and I would have marketing already built for those future albums. Later I decided that the first album should be Dan'l's Greatest Hits (Volume II) with everyone wanting to know how to get Volume I (which I would cut at a letter date). So it is with this book... if I am successful with 31 Best Practices Every Trainer Should Know (Vol. II), I will start on 31 Best Practices Every Trainer Should Know (Vol. I)!

Each chapter is made up of a suggested Best Practice, followed by a practical question or instruction and then an opportunity for you to set a goal for yourself to use the Best Practice. Take the time to think about each practice, answer the question, and then think how you can apply the practice in your own training profession.

Please join me as I share Best Practices one at a time….

DAN'L

Contents

Best Practice #1:

Prepare a Training Kit

I go around to each training with a small backpack (or a large day pack) which transports my PC, power cord, and projector connection. As an Eagle Scout, I also come prepared (Be Prepared is the Boy Scout motto). I bring with me a remote control for my PC... and extra AAA batteries for that remote. I bring pens, post-its, markers (wet and dry-erase), paper clips, 3x5 cards, a tablet of 8x10 paper, business cards, a small flashlight, a red pencil, blue painters tape (doesn't leave a mark on walls), extra paper copies of my presentation, and ...aspirin!

I once asked my manager to approve for me to order an additional light for my projector. She told me it wasn't necessary since the light lasted about 3,000 hours and I would never need it. Guess what happened within one month? Though I do not carry the extra light with me (they are hard to travel safely with), I do have one at the office ready to replace for the "next" presentation, instead of waiting for it to be shipped to me or taking the chance I cannot replace it at a local store. If your light goes out on your projector you have the great opportunity to train the (very) old fashioned way... without Power Point!

What additional items should you carry in your Training Kit?

Best Practice Goal #1: _____

Best Practice #2:

Take (and Use) Your Own Photos

In this day and age, your legal department may have concerns about your use of photos. Are they copyrighted? You may have a concern about whether the photo you would like to use really shows what you want it to show.

Nothing beats going out on your own and taking your own photo. You are the "owner" of that photo. Are you doing a presentation on construction? Take a photo at your own home or go out and take a few photos at a construction site (don't trespass!). How about some "vacation" pictures you have of famous buildings as you discuss construction techniques? Are you doing a presentation on auto claims? Go out and take a picture of your own auto or, maybe better yet, go to the auto junk yard!

Do you have additional ideas? Go out, take a picture, and include it in your next presentation.

Best Practice Goal #2: _____

Best Practice #3:

Pre-Assignment

There is some legitimate debate whether or not a trainer should assign a Pre-Assignment to a student before class ever begins. For those students who are taking CE (continuing education) type classes they may feel that this is additional work that they are not getting (CE) credit for. That is true. They may feel they do not have time for "extra" work.

My feeling is that for those who truly want to learn something, this is a good use of their time. It gives you the "edge" in the training you offer. The student gets more for their buck. It also underscores the seriousness and importance of your class. The pre-assignment brings everyone to the class at the same level... at least in theory. The secret however, is to assign just enough ahead of time to give the student real "meat" prior to the class that they can use to build on during the class. Do not give them too much where they get bored, scared, or feel it is only busy work. Explain the *purpose* of the assignment. Do not give them so much that they decide they really do not need to attend your class. Keep reading material down to the size of the average magazine article (2-3 pages).

If you have an activity for them to complete, make it short. A couple of thought provoking questions. Have them bring the completed pre-work to class... and then use it. If you are teaching about property insurance coverage to agents, ask them to think of a client whose claim was denied. When they arrive you can discuss their claim and why it wasn't covered and how it may be in the future. If teaching a new property claims adjuster, ask them to measure their backyard fence. And then discuss how to adjust for a fence claim. If you are teaching new entrepreneurs or business owners, ask them to think about what keeps them up at night. And then have them share those concerns with the class.

What Pre-Assignment work could you incorporate in the classes you offer?

Best Practice Goal #3: _____

Best Practice #4:

Market Yourself

There are lots of classes out there that a potential student can take. Some have a cost and some do not. Some offer Continuing Education (CE) credits and some do not. Some are live and some are not. Some have YOU as the course instructor and some do not! Why should anyone take a class from YOU?

I know that the class is supposed to be about the subject matter and not about you (it's not a Popularity Contest!)… but a student wants to know that their instructor is knowledgeable about the topic advertised. Do you not only talk the walk but can you also walk the walk? What experience have you had as a subject matter expert AND as an adult learning trainer? A short biography of YOU should accompany every course description. By knowing a little about YOU the student becomes more comfortable and confident about the time (and money) they are about to expend on taking your class. A photo of you may be also helpful…but make sure it is semi-professional at least and not a shot of you at your cousins barbeque whopping it up!

I have included an example on the next page:

Dan'l Adams

Mr. Adams has 26 years of experience in the insurance industry including sales, marketing, and 19 years of experience in claims working his way up from an Inside Adjuster to General Adjuster to Claims Team Manager. His experience includes working as an Independent Catastrophe (CAT) Adjuster after Hurricane Fran in North Carolina as well as a carrier Claims Auditor in the aftermath of the Northridge Earthquake in California. He was Vice-President of US Claims Inc. He currently is the Training Manager for National Programs and Operations for a Fortune 100 insurance company.

Mr. Adams is a graduate of Diablo Valley College (AA), Brigham Young University (BS), and holds a Juris Doctorate (JD) from Golden Gate University. He holds the AIC, AIS, AU, CLP, CIIP, ITP, and FCLS professional designations.

He previously was a Professor of Business Law at a small college in central California.

He is a Board Member of The Society of Registered Professional Adjusters (RPA), as well as Vice-President for The Society of Insurance Trainers and Educators. He is a Past President of the Modesto Claims Association. Mr. Adams has been a guest speaker at several Claims Association meetings as well as a featured presenter at the Claims Conference of Northern California and several Big I Conferences.

What do you think should be mentioned in a trainer biography?

Best Practice Goal #4: _____

Best Practice #5:

Appearance

Working from home has a number of advantages. One is that you can work in your sweats (pj's, shorts, etc.). Another is you don't have to shave. Let's face it... you can even be a little tardy on taking the morning shower. Hey, just put on a ball cap and you're good to go for the day! Mark Twain however said: "Clothes make the man. Naked people have little or no influence on society."

As a professional trainer however, your image, and therefore your appearance, is important. You are the subject matter expert in the area you are training on. You are the person that has the information the audience wants. You not only are representing yourself, but the company you work for. You feel better and you boost your confidence. You should also show some respect for the client, the audience, you are presenting to. Don't get sucked up into what everyone else is wearing. Just because you are presenting at an annual conference located at a beach resort where all of the participants are wearing Aloha shirts, shorts, and sandals, doesn't mean you should. You shouldn't!

Some say you should dress one step above what your audience is wearing. That may be good advice generally, but I prefer to wear a standard *uniform*. Not like a policeman's uniform or that of the local fast food chain... but a standard type of clothing that I wear to all of my presentations. For me I wear a suit. I do this for several reasons:

1) I don't have to decide what I'm going to wear that day. It's a suit... period. I don't have to waste time on what I'm packing before I go. The decision has already been made. It's one less thing I have to worry about.

2) I project a professional image, no matter who my audience is. There is a certain amount of respect and acceptance when a presenter is well dressed. It gives off the appearance that I am confidant and knowledgeable.

3) If I am really overdressed... or if it is really hot... I can take off my jacket. Hey, I can even take off my tie and roll up my shirt sleeves if it is appropriate. But I start out wearing my suit.

When I first started my career in the 1980's I read the book _Dress For Success_ by John Molloy. Back then his book was directed predominately toward a male audience. I believe subsequent editions have included specific chapters for women. Though *Business Casual* has garnered a large acceptance in modern business practice, the book is a classic of not only *what* to wear, but how, grooming, and even basic body language techniques. It's about projecting confidence, professionalism, and knowledge.

Though what you wear is important, it's also important that your clothes are clean, your shoes are shined, and that you are well groomed. Avoid extremes in dress, grooming, and accessories. Wear what you want on the weekends... but *never* in front of an audience. Wear the *uniform* of a professional trainer. *Look* the part!

How do you want a presenter to dress when you attend training? How does it influence you?

Best Practice Goal #5:_____

Best Practice #6:

Get `em Involved Right Away!

There they are. Your audience. Sitting there. Some with their arms crossed. Looking at you... *staring* at you. Challenging you to *make them learn something* and *enjoy it!* There's only one thing to do... get 'em involved right away!

The sooner you take control of your audience... by giving them some control... the sooner you will relax, they will relax, and learning can begin to take place. There are a myriad of ways to get your audience participating right away. Have them write down their name on a name tag or name tent. Have a question card about a display in the room that they can look at and attempt to answer the question about the display... give a prize to the winning answer! Tell them there is a $20 bill under one of their chairs (and make sure someone is actually sitting on *that* chair and there is in fact $20 underneath). Watch how fast everyone stands up and turns over their chair!

Here's one I have had success and fun with: Post 2 cards on a wall (one card says 0% and the other 100%. They are separated on the wall by about 5 feet). Ask the audience a question about percentage (i.e. How much of this presentation will you remember in 3 days?). Supply them with Post-It notes. Let them guess a number, get out of their chair, and place their Post-It note on the wall between 0 and 100. The answer is not as important as the fact they got out of their chairs and *did* something (in my case, I did give them the answer at the end of the presentation).

Another tried and true (and sometime boring) way of getting everyone to participate is the self-introduction. "Hi, my name is Dan'l Adams and I work for blah, blah, blah...." (You're thinking "Will someone shut that guy up... just *shoot* me now!"). You can have each participant introduce themselves to the person sitting next to them and allow them to introduce each other. Really not much better than the self-introduction. What can you do? Think about it. We'll discuss in the next chapter.

What are some tips you would suggest to get your audience involved right away?

Best Practice Goal #6:_____

Best Practice #7:

Self Introductions

In Best Practice #6 we discussed how to get your students involved right away. We briefly discussed having them introduce themselves, or having the person next to them find out a little about them and then introduce them to the group. Depending on the size of your group this can get rather tedious and boring. "Heck! Why do I want to know about this guy anyway? I didn't come here today to make new friends. I came here today to learn something!"

This brings us to the very point of the matter…what is the real *purpose* of self-introductions?

Self-Introductions are a method of getting your students to participate right away. It gets them to get out of their chair and speak for a few seconds on something they are an expert about…themselves. Remember however, you are the master of ceremonies during this exercise in bragging. You are in control. So other than getting them to participate right away in your class, what are other reasons you want to participate in this costly practice that takes away from your instructional time?

One reason is you get a sense right away of who may participate and who may not. Some people LOVE to talk about themselves…and they do…on and on and on. Some barely get their name out before asking you "what did you want me to say again?" This brings up again that you are in charge of this ego fest. You set the ground rules before they begin. Give them an example of what you want. I have a slide that has the three or four items I want them to comment on. In fact, during a multi-day seminar, I will ask them to *draw* their responses on a piece of easel pad paper using color markers. For example:

On a piece of easel pad paper DRAW:

Your Name

How long in the Insurance Industry

Favorite Sports Team

Something you like to do when not selling insurance

I personally set the example by starting out the discussion with some information about myself (including having a good personal story – we'll discuss next during Best Practice # 8)…and yes I even draw a picture of the requested information. The purpose of self-introductions will be different for a 2 hour Continuing Education class versus a week long seminar. For a multi-day workshop or seminar it is important for the students to bond right away. This assists them later when starting on a team building exercise or small team discussion (where they would have introduced themselves anyway).

The self-introduction allows me a method of knowing who may have participated in a pre-work assignment: "After giving us your name and agency you work for, tell us what example from the pre-reading affected you the most." The self-introduction can allow me to find out what experience they have: "Tell us how long have you been in the insurance industry and what your specialty is?"

On a multi-day course, it allows me an opportunity to have an "in" with my student. It allows me an opportunity to have something that I can begin a discussion with them about before going into a discussion about the class itself. It is a trust builder. The student knows that I care about them as a person first…and then as a student. I now become a trusted resource and not just a lecturer.

What purpose would you have for having your students give a self-introduction?

Best Practice Goal #7:_____

Best Practice #8:

Have a Good Personal Story

In Best Practice #7 we discussed the value of self-introductions. I brought up the fact that I, myself, give a self-introduction as an example. I then continue with a personal story. Depending on the audience it may be more professionally focused or actually about my personal life. Let's explore the difference:

Professionally Focused

If my subject matter for the day is more technically oriented, such as a discussion on the exclusions found in an insurance policy's coverage and what endorsements may provide coverage back to fill that gap, the audience may want to know why they should listen to me. What makes me an expert in the subject that I will be teaching them on today? This is where it is fine to briefly discuss your background as far as education and experience. If you are talking to a group of insurance agents, let them know that you sold insurance. If you are talking to a group of insurance adjusters let them know you have your Associate in Claims (AIC) designation.

Be careful however. You don't want to sound like you are bragging. I get through that hurdle by telling a story:

It just so happens that before I began my insurance career (1989) I was managing a small retail store in a mall in the San Francisco Bay Area. I usually worked late hours, but on this day…which happened to be Opening Day of the World Series between the two Bay Area teams (The Oakland A's and the San Francisco Giants), I had completed my work and was going to come home at a decent time. I called my wife to let her know I was coming home. While on the phone the store started rattling and swaying as the Loma Prieta Earthquake started. I threw down my phone as the shelves above my desk, full of glassware, collapsed onto my desk.

Did it catch your interest? Do you want to know more? I continue with the story including that a month later I left retail management and began my career as an insurance adjuster. There is a tie in between the story (a significant natural catastrophe and wide spread damage) and the beginning of a career helping others as an insurance adjuster. I can then go into a brief description of my career (which in fact included the Oakland fire storm just a few years later; another Earthquake, and Hurricane Fran that hit North Carolina in 1996). The story peaks their interest and at the same time validates me as an insurance professional.

Personally Focused

I have found that often times, when in front of my training peers, or to lighten the mood a bit, I start off with a more personal story. One about how I got into training. I let people into my own personal world as I talk about the birth of my 2nd grandchild. I talk about how, with tears running down her face, my wife asked me "couldn't you get a transfer?" as we're in the airport traveling back to our home 2 states away. I talk about how it seemed like miracles were occurring as my predecessor was retiring, I got the job, and we were able to relocate from California to Washington State. I talk about living with my daughters family for 3 months as I started my new position and my wife had to stay back to sell our home. I talk about how my grandchildren got to know me as I lived with them and that now they call me Gampy, or even sometimes refer to me as "The Gampster" (as I puff out my chest because to me it sounds like they think I'm a super hero).

The group smiles (and even chuckles at the super hero reference) and a connection between trainer and class has occurred.

And that was the point…to make a connection: I'm one of you and I have something that you're going to want to hear. As their interest has now peaked, they give me their full attention as I begin the first session of their training.

What personal story can you tell that relates to a training delivery you are giving?

Best Practice Goal #8:_____

Best Practice #9:

So What?

For years I started every training session I had, whether it was a Sunday school class, a Scout Leader training, or a professional presentation with this question: *So What?*

Now this isn't the "so what?" response you may get from your children when they have done something wrong and you put them in *time out.* This is the *KEY* question every student should ask themselves when taking a class, attending a presentation, or reading an article: So What? So what does this class have to do with me? So what does this presentation have to do with my job? So what does this article mean to me and how I can be a better_____ (fill in the blank: manager, producer, father, etc.)?

Every student should have an inner conversation with themselves before, during, and after every education opportunity (including YOUR training session with them) on what that time should mean to them. What is the benefit they will get? They need to come prepared. Prepared to have the desire to learn. They need to come to the training with the right attitude. How many of you have ever had a student who seemed to be leaning back in their chair with their arms crossed and staring you down as if to say "Go ahead…try to *teach* me something…I *dare* you! Without the right attitude, without the right inner preparation, without the right *desire*…learning will not…and cannot take place!

Remind your students early on that learning is a team effort…you will bring the information…but they need to bring the desire to learn.

Bottom line is this: They are responsible for their own development. They need to be able to incorporate their learning of today into their actions of tomorrow. They need to be able to answer the question *So What?* So what does this have to do with me?

What can you do to encourage your participants to personalize the training you are presenting? How can you encourage them to answer *"So What?"* for themselves?

Best Practice Goal #9:_____

Pre-Training Quiz

What is the real purpose of training? To show others what you, the instructor, knows? To share a bunch of information that just fills up a bunch of someone else's valuable time so they can get some continuing education (CE) credits? No... the purpose of training is to help others fill in the gaps of their knowledge to help them become better in whatever they do. To do this, we must determine what the student already knows. We must find out what the knowledge gaps are...and then teach to fill the gaps!

This certainly will mean extra work for you as an instructor... but it also means you will become the kind of instructor that presents meaningful information to their students and is respectful of their time. To do this, prepare a Pre-Knowledge Quiz.

<u>Give at the beginning of class:</u> I have done this when I knew I was going to teach some pretty technical information (such as policy endorsements or state laws) and wanted to show an improvement of knowledge to the students between what they knew before class and what they knew at the conclusion of the class. I hand out a simple 10 question, multiple choice quiz. I instruct them to not guess at any of the answers...they either know the correct answer and mark it, or leave it blank. After they take the Pre-Quiz I ask how many they THINK they got right. This can be an eye opener and a fun part of the class. Several times I have *old-timers* readily admit that they

don't know the answers which then put everyone else in the class at ease. Normally I get no one in the class answer more than 5 or 6 (out of 10) correctly. This allows the entire class to pay more attention to my presentation because they know I will be speaking to *a gap that they themselves have identified.* I then use the quiz during the course of the instruction to make sure I cover all of the points. I usually don't give the quiz again, but you certainly can to use as an evaluation of the knowledge that was gathered during the class. Compare how many got the questions right at the beginning of the class to how many they got right at the conclusion of the class. This confirms to the students that the class was indeed a valuable use of their time.

<u>Send out the Pre-Quiz ahead of time</u>: Honestly however, if you are going to teach to the students gaps, you need to know where the gaps are ahead of time and adjust your presentation accordingly. This takes time, this takes effort. But you will be accomplishing a lot more for your students benefit if you take the time, ahead of time, to know what their pre-class knowledge is. The quiz does not have to be elaborate. Again, I would suggest a simple 10 question, multiple choice answer quiz, that cover the high points of your presentation. If everyone gets one of the questions right, you know not to waste valuable class time teaching on that subject. Spend more time teaching on the questions (subjects) that everyone (or mostly everyone) missed. Word of caution here…just as in Scouting, where you hike to the speed of your slowest hiker (so they won't get lost), teach to the knowledge of any of your students who get a question wrong (so they won't get lost) – in other words, if one person misses the question, teach the concept.

What do you think is best…sending out the Pre-Quiz ahead of time or at the beginning of class? Develop a Pre-Training Quiz for one of your classes.

Best Practice Goal #10:_____

Best Practice #11:

Align Objectives With Assessments

I am amazed at how many trainings start without informing the student what the objectives of the training are. How does the student know that he has been successful in learning what was meant to be taught that day? Even more amazing is the fact that there is not an assessment at the end of the training. Again, how does the student know that he learned what was meant to be taught? How does the instructor know if learning has actually taken place? I guess one could think that without a map (objectives), it doesn't really matter where you end up (or what you have learned or not learned)!

More troubling however is when *objectives* are shared and *assessments* are given, but they do not align. In other words the assessment does not test the knowledge that the objective advertised at the beginning of the class. Let me share an example:

Objective: Upon completion of the course the student will be able to list the property coverage's included in the ISO Basic Property form.

Non- Aligned Assessment: What does the acronym FLARE stand for?

Aligned Assessment: List the property coverage's included in the ISO Basic Property form.

Note that the non-aligned assessment has nothing to do with

the objective. It may have been taught, it may be important, but it in no way aligns with the stated purpose, or *objective.* When assessments align with objectives the teacher *and* the learner can recognize when the proscribed learning has 1) been taught and 2) has been learned. Also note how *easy* it was to come up with the assessment…it almost exactly follows the objective word for word!

One other value of having and aligning assessments to objectives supports the old teaching method of 1) this is what I'm going to teach you (objective) 2) this is what I'm teaching you (delivery) and 3) this is what I taught you (assessment).

Develop an aligned assessment with an objective for a future class you will be teaching, or designing, soon.

Best Practice Goal #11:_____

Have a Partner

There is the old adage that two heads are better than one. Mother Teresa said "I can do what you can't do, and you can do what I can't do. *Together* we can do great things." Nowhere does that seem more appropriate than in the training field.

I enjoy public speaking. I enjoy making presentations to a live crowd. It's a thrill for me that I look forward to. But ask me to conduct a webinar, and I all but freeze up. How do I sign on? What do I do if I lose the connection? Are the participants paying attention? What if there was a fire drill in the building I'm at (it really happened on a webinar I was presenting in 2011!)? I get anxious and become a nervous wreck the couple of days before the webinar. I have found however, that if I have a co-presenter, a *partner,* I become less anxious and less nervous than if I were going it solo. I know some of you feel the same way when presenting in person. The presentation partner that I have may be a Subject Matter Expert (SME) during a live presentation or they may be more skilled handling the Informational Technology (IT) aspect of the webinar. They can co-host and handle subject matter questions I don't have the answers for. They can handle the technology of the webinar...the signing in of registrants, the handling of the chat room answering questions, troubleshooting when something goes wrong during the call.

A partner is also beneficial as you prepare for your presentation. A partner can be someone that can edit your presentation for grammar or as a fact checker. A partner can be someone who will listen to a practice delivery. A partner can be someone you trust who will be honest with you and let you know what you can do to present a better presentation…and frankly, look better in the eyes of your students.

A partner can help you make a better presentation, strengthen you where you have a weakness, and overall make you look better to your audience. A point to remember however…you are now *their* partner and are under the same obligation to help them make a better presentation, to strengthen them where they have a weakness, and overall to make them look better in front of their audience…which just so happens is the same audience that you have, the one that the two of you share together. A good partner is a good friend to have!

Recruit a partner to assist you in giving your next presentation. Who will you ask? Why? What will you ask them to do?

Best Practice Goal #12:_____

Best Practice #13:

Body Language Awareness

I sometimes take a bus into the city. For a while I found that, most of the time, I was the last one on the bus that anyone sat next to. For a long time I really felt bad. Was I that ugly? Did I smell? I didn't know why no one was sitting next to me. About this time I was doing some research on Body Language Awareness. I read about how a person crossing their arms, with both hands tucked into their body gave off a negative vibe. By their body actions they were saying don't even think about coming close to me or saying anything to me. That was it! That's why no one sat next to me! That's how I sat on the bus. So what did I do from then on? I sat exactly the same way with my arms crossed and both hands tucked in! I didn't want anyone to sit next to me anyway!

55% of all communication is non-verbal…body language. A person's body language is an art form to be studied and to be aware of. I say art form, because it is not really a science. Oh we know that *usually* crossed arms, as used in my example above, mean that a person is standoffish, maybe even unapproachable…but not necessarily. It might just be that is a favorite resting position or he doesn't know what to do with his arms.

One body action, in and of itself, may mean nothing. But several, taken together, may be sending a very clear message. A student crosses his arms, leans back in his chair, and then yawns may mean that your presentation isn't going too well.

He's bored. He's challenging you, daring you "Go ahead TRY to teach me something." At the same time, you, the presenter, standing behind a speaker's podium, with your hands in your pockets and trying to take that coy look at the clock on the wall gives just as clear of a message to your students that you would rather be somewhere else. And that's something you need to be aware of! Your own body language!

You need to be aware of the 5 areas of the body that give off signals: personal space; body angle; face; arms; legs. There are several books written about body language. I would suggest reading one that gives you an overall view of what certain body movements *may* mean. Being aware of your student's body language, as well as your own, is critical for your success as a trainer.

Have a partner watch you during your next presentation and write down what they observe of your body language.

Best Practice Goal #13:_____

Best Practice #14:

Expect Audience Participation

One of the great fears of a trainer is presenting in front of an audience. Will they pay attention? Will they like me? Will they like my presentation? What if they don't participate? Though the fear of public speaking is the #1 fear of most people…you should not let it overly worry you. Your students are there at your presentation for a reason. They are there because they want to learn something. Or they are there because of your reputation as a speaker or presenter. Honestly, some may be there because they need the Continuing Education credits…but they might as well get something out of the time they are there. Those who have spent money to attend your class really want to get something out of it. They don't want to feel like they wasted their hard earned dollars (and their boss doesn't want to feel like they wasted *their* hard earned dollars if paying for the student to attend). Remember this…just as you may have a fear of speaking in public (and you're a professional speaker or trainer!), your student probably has that same fear!

I expect my audience to participate. Why? Because I have *planned* for their participation. I plan small group discussions with a member of the group reporting back to the class what was discussed. I just don't ask for volunteers to help me with a flipchart or for a response to a question, I ask a specific person to help me or to respond to my question. I look them in the eye and ask them! I plan for the groups to play short games to get them out of their chairs and participate. I have even taped a $20 bill to the bottom of one of the chairs in the room to get everyone up and moving (see Best Practice # 6). The secret of audience participation is that you as the instructor have *planned* it to occur. When you *plan* audience participation you can *expect* audience participation.

What will you do at your next training to enhance audience participation? How will you plan it?

Best Practice Goal #14:_____

Best Practice #15:

Small Groups

There never seems to be enough time to teach on everything that you would like during a class session. There always seems to be one or two class participants that want to control the show…thinking their comments are the only valid comments that should be heard.

A little maturity has convinced me that in all actuality I do not know everything. Far from it. In fact, part of the joy I get from facilitating a class is learning something new from someone else. There is an old saying: Two heads are better than one. In this case, several small groups are better than one large one.

Separating your class into several small groups accomplishes a few things: 1) It allows students to interact with each other; 2) more points of view can come into the limelight; 3) several mini-topics can be addressed at once.

1) It allows students to interact with each other. Many students have the same fear as most of us…public speaking. Many do not wish to say something in front of a large group of people…and certainly not in front of the instructor! Most, however, will gain some courage if the group has reduced in size AND the instructor is not part of the group. Now they can test their comments in a safer environment with just a few people sitting around a table.

2) More points of view can come into the limelight. There will always be those few in a class who want to dominate the conversation. Let's face it…they will still dominate the conversation in the small group too…but they will not dominate the *entire* class leaving others in the small groups they are not in a better chance to voice their opinion and make their comments.

3) Several mini-topics can be addressed at once. Separating into smaller groups for group discussion is a great way to handle the situation when several examples of a learning point need to be addressed. Let each table discuss a different set of facts and let them determine how to apply the learning point you taught in the class. At the end, let a spokesman relate the facts that they discussed and share with the larger group the review and answer the small group came up with.

A word of warning. Give yourself enough time to wander through each of the groups and listen to their discussion. Keep them on track and provide necessary course corrections if necessary. This may be in the form of a provocative question or point of clarification. Remember to allow enough time for the small groups to report their discussion and findings.

How will you use small group work during your next training?

Best Practice Goal #15:_____

Best Practice #16:

K.I.S.S.

When I first heard of this acronym several years ago, it had somewhat of a negative message. I was therefore surprised when I heard it used in church a couple of years ago…until the speaker defined it…Keep It Simply SIMPLE!

Many times we go overboard in our preparation…this causes anxiety…sometimes even sickness. K.I.S.S. is a powerful principle to understand, use and enjoy. Keep your presentations simply simple! We have all heard of Death by PowerPoint. Don't do it! If you can say your message in a few minutes rather than an hour - do it! If you can say it in a few seconds than a few minutes – do it! And if I will take my own advice…this Best Practice tip ends now! K.I.S.S.

What will you do at your next training differently to Keep It Simply Simple?

Best Practice Goal #16:_____

Best Practice #17:

Write and Share

Have you ever heard the phrase "Two heads are better than one?" This Best Practice underscores this teaching.

This works well where you have your students sitting at a common table. During the training I will supply each person a blank sheet of paper. I ask them to write one thing they know about a subject. Then I ask them to give the paper to the person sitting on their right and ask that they again repeat the process of writing down the SAME thing they did on the first paper...with this warning...only as long as it has not been previously written down. If previously written they need to come up with a new comment. I ask them to repeat the cycle until everyone at the table has had a chance to write a comment on the same common subject. Now everyone has a sheet of paper with different comments on a subject. This works especially well as a review or to provide a summary of a teaching you had made.

Let me share an example. If I had students sitting in round tables of six and I had taught about George Washington a Write and Share paper may end up looking like this:

1. George Washington was a general.

2. He was our first President

3. He was President of the Constitutional Convention

4. He owned a lot of property in Virginia

5. His wife was Martha

6. He traveled once outside of the United States to Bermuda with his older brother

This may seem pretty simple. The concept though is that now the student has 6 facts that he/she can use if they were asked to speak about George Washington. The one comment that they wrote over and over they have certainly memorized, and, they have a summary of what you taught that day.

What presentation point in your next training will you challenge your students to Write and Share?

Best Practice Goal #17_____

Best Practice #18:

Use Take-Away Cards

Closely akin to our #17 Best Practice of Write and Share, is the best practice of using Take-Away cards during your training.

This is a simple practice with nothing more than supplying a 3x5 card at each student's seat at the start of your presentation (I prefer the color 3x5 cards myself). Why? I'll be quite honest with you. I'm pretty lazy when I go to a training. I don't bring a binder (too bulky) and I don't intend to make any notes (that would imply that I was going to read my notes later). But I always find that if there is a small piece of paper and a pen in front of me I invariably will take a note or two (I loved that funny quote! What was the reference for the YouTube video? That's a great idea to use at my next team meeting.). On top of that...a 3x5 card is so transportable! I can slip it in my pocket at the end of the session and no one knows anything different...and if the truth be known, I will take it out later and read it. And if you are going to use the Write and Share tip, you need to supply the cards anyway. WOW! Using 2 tips all at once! You're becoming a Master Trainer!

How will you use Take-Away cards during your next training?

Best Practice Goal #18_____

Best Practice #19:

Use Small Handouts

I love Freebies! I love SWAG (little giveaways often handed out at vendor booths at trade shows with their corporate name/logo on them)! I collect all of them…they're great to give the grandkids!

Face it however, if I'm not giving them away I'm throwing them away when I get back to the office. How many stress balls, pens and post-it notes do I need? Plus, I have the SWAG my own company produces. I don't need more stuff.

We've already discussed how I don't like to take notes… that implies I'm going to go back to my home or office and read it. It's not going to happen. The same with a multi-page handout that is a copy of the presenter's notes or his slide show. Believe me…I will glance at it for 10seconds before it is filed away…and probably filed away in the circular can!

Don't get me wrong. I appreciate that I was given something. It makes me feel that I got more for my money…it's just that ultimately it's going to be filed away one way or another.

I recently heard a speaker at a conference. I enjoyed what the speaker had to say. So much so, I bought her book…I even had her sign it. And here it sits at my desk …unopened and unread!

What I do need though is a *small* take-away tool, a *small* hand out, a *small* training aid *that* will jog my memory on what I learned in the class that day. Note that I emphasized the word *small*. If what you are teaching is worthwhile, you can probably still narrow down your main points to the size of a 3X5 card…or less! I've seen some very effective wallet size reminder cards…in fact I've kept a couple of them! Some I have even taken out of my wallet and placed where I will need them most…at my desk or on my computer. Where I can *see* them and *use* them. Where they can jog my memory to the message that was presented at the training.

Remember the speaker whose book I haven't read? What I do have and what I have referred to several times since the conference is a small handout she had left on each table. I'm looking at it right now sitting on my desk! Heavy card stock…a little bigger than a dollar bill. Will it be there forever? No…it will be replaced…but only after I have viewed it several times, being reminded of the speaker's message weeks or months after her presentation. By then, I may have even absorbed some of her message into my way of thinking and doing things. Is that not what you want your training to do? Don't you want your students to *remember* and *use* the information you provided in your training? Then give them something worthwhile…a *small* handout.

What *small*, worthwhile, handout will you give out at your next training?

Best Practice Goal #19_____

Best Practice #20:

Flip Chart Usage

Flip Charts? That's so old school!

Is it? Don't tell your students that…and don't sell this valuable training tool short! If you want to get group participation…especially small group participation, this is the tool to use! Here are some tips for its use:

1. Parking Lot – there are times you just didn't figure on mentioning something in your training that others want to discuss. They ask you a question in the middle of your presentation. Do you stop and get off track? No, you respond with "That's a very good question…let's put it on our flip chart here to remind us to talk about this later today." Make sure you do come back to it later!

2. Blank – You start with a blank piece of flip chart paper. You ask the class a question and record their responses (better yet, ask a student to come up and record for you). This gets the class thinking and participating. This is a great ice breaker. Personally I like using the "Post It" style of flip chart paper with the sticky backing. That way, when I fill a page, I can tear it off, and then post it on the wall. WARNING: Best Practice Tip – Only use the top 2/3 of the page. Many facilitators try to cram too much on one page and start writing smaller and smaller…and frankly messier and messier. They want to get it all on a single page. Don't do that! Another factor is that many in the back of

the class cannot see the bottom 1/3 of the page from where they are sitting.

3. Prepared Visual Tool- I often have a prepared quote or data on my flip chart. I keep a couple of blank pages in front to cover it up until I'm ready to use it (hint: I tag the pages on the side with post it notes to easily find the page when I need it). Unless you are writing responses directly from the audience, never write on the flip chart during class. Prepare beforehand. Otherwise you are turning your back on your students and they become disengaged. Use the flip chart as an additional tool to highlight a thought you are sharing. Remember – most people respond more to visual triggers than just lecture.

4. Small Group Recording Tool- I often supply a flip chart at each small group table at my training. I give the group a question/assignment to discuss and then have them record their responses…and then have them teach back to the rest of the class.

5. Reminder – One of the reasons I like using Post It flip charts is to keep the back of the chart clear. Why? I tape my class agenda on the back. I tape key points to the back. That way I don't have to carry my notes with me or go back to the podium. I just sneak a peek at the back of the flip chart! Take that Power Point!

How will you use a flipchart at your next training?

Best Practice Goal #20_____

Best Practice #21:

Use Multiple Visual Aids

People learn in different ways. Some by listening; some by seeing, some by doing. However most adult education professionals agree that better learning takes place when the instructor uses various training methods to teach a subject. An additional visual aid is one of the most effective learning methods an instructor can use. By using visual aids, the instructor reinforces his lecture. There are a myriad of visual aids. In the last chapter we talked about using a flip chart. In previous chapters we have discussed photos, take away cards, and even SWAG. Add to that books, training manuals, posters, and product examples. And lest we forget...the powerful Power Point presentation.

What visual aid will you use in your next training?

Best Practice Goal #21:_____

Best Practice #22:

Know Your Slides

We've all heard about it. You have probably attended them. Hopefully you have never done it yourself. Lecture from the Power Point slides themselves (Death by Power Point). This is caused for one of two reasons (or both!). The Instructional Designer tried to put every detail in the slide itself (and therefore there is nothing else for the Trainer to do than read the slide) or the Trainer does not know their subject (or is scared of the audience and won't look at them) and relies totally on what is up on the slide screen.

Though a separate subject, good slide construction is important. It should be used to emphasize a point to the student or in the worst case scenario as a memory jog for the instructor to keep him on track.

A good instructor should come prepared. They should know what they are teaching. They should know the order in which they are teaching. They should know what Point B is, that it follows Point A, and precedes Point C. They should not have to guess what is on the next slide, or even what the slide is about. In a pinch they should be able to look at the slide to get oriented where they are in the presentation, then turn away and address their audience. DO NOT READ FROM THE SLIDE!

How can I do a better job NOT relying on my slide presentation?

Best Practice Goal #22: _____

Best Practice #23:

Slow Down!

"What did she just say?" "Did you get that?" "What was the third point mentioned?"

We've all been in those classes before where the speaker is going so fast we can't keep up! We're trying to pay attention. The information is darn great. We're trying to take notes. The speaker is just speaking faster than we are writing. What's worse, he spent the time to show us a slide and then Whoosh! It's gone. You didn't get half way through copying down the slide (by the way, is the instructor going to give us a copy of his slide deck?).

The answer to all of this of course is for you as the speaker to SLOW DOWN! This isn't a horse race. There is no reward for ending early (in fact you may be penalized if you finish early, especially if you are awarding continuing education credits). Take your time. Relax a bit. Let the students actually learn something by pondering what you have said instead of going from point to point to point.

How do you slow down?

Slow down your pace and your delivery. Slow down your speech. Pause between new points. Take a sip of water (or my favorite, a Diet Dr. Pepper). Restate a point in a different way…or just repeat it again for emphasis. Ask questions of the students ("how would you apply that last point to your present job?"). Ask "am I going too fast?"

You may say that you will never get through all of the material. That's ok. What you actually want is for learning to take place. You want the students to enjoy your presentation and get something out of it. The one thing your student doesn't want is to feel stressed, confused, and uptight. Because at the end of the day, if they do, they will blame you!

How will I slow down my next presentation?

Best Practice Goal #23: _____

Best Practice #24:

Prepare the Student for the Question

I have been in classes where the instructor has asked me a question. For whatever reason I was not prepared for the question. Has that ever happened to you? I might have been daydreaming, reading ahead in the syllabus, thinking about the last point made, or maybe, I just wasn't getting it. But for whatever reason, I was asked a question and I was dumbfounded. What's more I was embarrassed…and you know what? So was the instructor!

To prevent embarrassing the student (and myself!) I have learned to prepare the student for the question. Whether you are live or on a webinar, simply telling the student ahead of time that you will call on them next is a great presentation tool. Simply say "John, I'm going to ask you a question concerning the next point. I want you to think about how you might apply it in your day to day sales activity" or something like that. Then, proceed with the point you were about to make and then ask John the question. By preparing John beforehand, you have allowed him to be more focused on what you are talking about, allows him to think ahead on how he might respond, and prevents an awkward moment in your class. It does something else too! It lets other students know that from time to time, you might ask them a question about what you are talking about…and they better pay attention!

I have also used this method to control the know-it all

student from blurting out a response (someone else is getting a turn), bring out a non-participating student from their shell, or assist in controlling the trouble maker by allowing him to talk…but when I say so.

Remember to RECOGNIZE the student afterward. Compliment their response. Maybe they have given some good insight or example. You should at least be able to thank them for participating in the class.

What happens when you prepare a student, and they still can't answer you because they still don't understand? This is a gift! You can certainly ask for someone else's response but it may be a hint to you that you have not explained the point satisfactorily. Work with the student(s) then to see what you can do to teach the concept better.

What will I do different in my presentations to prepare students for an upcoming question?

Best Practice Goal #24: _____

Best Practice #25:

What Did You Learn Today?

At the end of each training I ask students to fill out an evaluation (we will discuss this more in Best Practice #26 – Move Up to a Level 2 (or level 3) Evaluation). Part of the evaluation is to ask the student, what did you learn? Many times I have been on the receiving end of that question. I know I learned a lot (what was that idea the trainer shared during the first hour?), but frankly it is at the end of the day…I want to go home. My brain is fried. I can't, or won't, think any more…at least if I have to recall something from 8 hours ago. And so I have often left that portion of the evaluation blank. How as a trainer then do I learn from that and make it easy for my students to recall what they learned and put it in writing on the evaluation form? I ask them!

I ask them throughout the day. I ask them at the end of each module. What did you learn in this last hour? How will you apply it to your job when you get home. WRITE IT DOWN. Now we can take our 10 minute break.

I get them to commit after each learning session. I have them think while it is fresh in their minds. I have them write it down. At the end of the day they will have a record of what they learned and how they will apply it. It gives them a final learning application that allows them, for just a few minutes, to actually think about what and how they can apply to what was just shared with them. They take ownership for a portion of their learning during the day. They can answer, what's in it for me? They can now fill out the final evaluation form…and what's more have something to refer to when their boss asks "Did you learn anything at the training?"

When will I ask the question "What did you learn?" during my next presentation?

Best Practice Goal #25: _____

Best Practice #26:

Move Up to a Level 2 (or 3) Evaluation

Most trainers know about Kirkpatrick's four levels of evaluation. In brief:

Level 1 – Reaction, which measures how participants like the training (and/or the instructor). We have often referred these evaluations as "smile sheets" because most students just want to check off a box quickly and will usually give the instructor and class a good score

Level 2 – Learning, which measures what participants have learned from the training. Often this is done through some pre and post testing (see Best Practice #10 – Pre-Training Quiz).

Level 3 – Behavior, which measures whether the student is actually applying what was learned at the training to his actual job.

Level 4 – Results, which measures whether the application of training is actually achieving some type of noticeable results (increase in sales, increase in income, increase in attendance etc.).

While many trainers and their companies are satisfied with the *smile sheets*, they only inform the trainer and his manager that the students *LIKED* the training. Heck, if you feed me a great lunch and include a lot of snacks, what's there not to like?

The real challenge is to make sure you, as the trainer, really did your job. Did the student actually *LEARN* something in the training (level 2)? Asking questions throughout the training asking the participant *what did you learn?* (Best Practice #25) will be invaluable at the end of the training in underscoring to the student that yes, indeed, he did learn something at the course and it was not a complete waste of time (other than the Great lunch!). Using a test at the end of the training with questions that match favorably (or exactly) with a pre-training test will show immediately the increase in the students' knowledge (at least short term).

How could you increase that learning curve even more and have the student show that they can apply the learning to the real world (level 3)? How about roll play? Better yet, if you are learning sales techniques, provide the student with a few leads and have them get on their cell phone and do some cold calling. They get the practice, you can observe and critique, and their confidence builds!

The increased level of evaluation not only helps you to know how your training went but actually is another training tool to help the student embed the training they took that day.

What question(s) (or activity) will I add to my current evaluation to move it from a level 1 evaluation to a level 2 evaluation (or from a level 2 evaluation to a level 3 evaluation)?

Best Practice Goal #26: _____

Best Practice #27:

Encourage Students to Keep a Journal

Wouldn't it be great if your student kept learning after your presentation? Wouldn't it be great if they were able to apply what they learned? Wouldn't it be great if they took some responsibility for their continued growth...and kept track of it? Kept track of additional resources. Kept track of the additional thoughts after the training that naturally come while they are driving back home that day. Kept track of what went well and what didn't when they tried to use their new learnings on the job.

Challenge your students to the above. Challenge them to keep track in a training or work journal. It doesn't have to be fancy. They can keep notes in a 3 ring binder; in a spiral notebook, or on a journal app on their phone or tablet. The idea is for them to record ideas as they have them and to think about how to use those ideas at work...and then record their results! Over time they will be able to determine positively if the training you shared with them was of any benefit...and by how much! They will be surprised at how much additional learning and development will take place if they continue with this additional learning tool.

What will I share with the student about the benefits of keeping a post training journal?

Best Practice Goal #27: _____

Best Practice #28:

Learn From Others

I wish I could say that I knew it all. I may act that way sometimes, but in all actuality I don't know everything. That's when I need to rely upon the knowledge of others. Training skills are no exception. That's why you're reading this book isn't it? Because you thought that maybe I knew something more than you. To be honest most, if not all, of the tips found in this book were from what I learned from others over time.

Continue to ask for tips from other trainers. Observe them in action. What do they do well? What do they do not so well? I encourage you to keep notes on your computer or in a journal. Practice what you learned at your next presentation. You should live what you teach…improve on your skills and be a lifelong student of learning and improving.

Who will I ask for training tips?

Best Practice Goal #28: _____

Best Practice #29:

What Are My Best Ideas?

I hope you have enjoyed this book and will be able to put a few of these tips into practical use as a trainer. I have left the last 3 training tips blank for you to put in favorite tips from other trainers or ones that you have developed yourself. You too have experience as a trainer whether you know it or not. In fact, I bet I could learn something from you! I would love to hear from you! Send your tips to me at danl_adams@yahoo.com.

Best wishes in your continued success as a trainer. Remember, people are coming to you for training. You're going to continue to be GREAT!

What training tip have I picked up from other trainers or from my own experience?

Best Practice Goal #29: _____

Best Practice #30:

Insert a Best Practice Here:

How will I use the last Best Practice training tip in my next training?

Best Practice Goal #30: _____

Best Practice #31:

Insert a Best Practice Here:

How will I use the last Best Practice training tip in my next training?

Best Practice Goal #31: _____

Dan'l is a certified coach, trainer and speaker. He has earned the Certified Leadership Professional (CLP) and Insurance Training Professional (ITP) designations. He is a member of the board for both the Society of Insurance Trainers and Educators as well as the Society of Registered Professional Adjusters. Dan'l and his wife Carolyn live in the Pacific Northwest with their dog Tinkerbell Yoda. They have 3 children and 3 grandchildren (that's why they moved to the Pacific Northwest!).

You can contact Dan'l at danl_adams@yahoo.com to work with your trainers to become the BEST at what they do!